ENSURING ACADEMIC SUCCESS & YOUR GRADUATION

K. Sathasivan, PhD

Sentia Publishing Company, Lakeway, Texas

Copyright © 2020 by Kanagasabapathi Sathasivan

Sentia Publishing
831 Sunfish St.
Lakeway, TX 78734

http://www.sentiapublishing.com/

Ordering Information:

Quantity sales. Special discounts are available on quantity purchases by universities, colleges, associations, and others. For details, contact the publisher at the address above.
Orders by U.S. trade bookstores, libraries and wholesalers. Please contact William England at (512) 784-7497

Printed in the United States of America

Publisher's Cataloging-in-Publication data
Kanagasabapathi Sathasivan
Book Title: Ensuring Academic Success & Your Graduation
ISBN: 978-1-7340764-5-5
The main category of the book 1. Education. Other categories: 2. Graduation, 3. Academic Success, 4. Student Retention, 5. Study Skills

First Edition

Dedicated to

my teachers, students, wife, and
children who taught me the real value of
education beyond what I knew.

CONTENTS

INTRODUCTION   1

UNIT 1. KNOWLEDGE   9

Chapter 1. Start with a Big Picture   10

Chapter 2. Connecting the Dots   15

Chapter 3. Application is Key   21

Personal Success Story 1 by Dr. Martin Perez, MD, MBA, FHM   26

Personal Success Story 2 by Mark Adkins, BA, JD   31

UNIT 2. STUDY SKILLS   39

Chapter 4. Art of Memorization   40

Chapter 5. Mechanisms of Learning   47

Chapter 6. Seven Principles of Smart Learning   55

Personal Success Story 3 by Dr. Fahmi Farah, MD   62

Personal Success Story 4 by Sriram Palepu, BSA, BBA   68

UNIT 3. MOTIVATION   73

Chapter 7. Beyond Grades   74

Chapter 8. Health Matters   79

Chapter 9. True Grit   85

Personal Success Story 5 by Omar Vayani, BSA   90

Personal Success Story 6 by Sailesh Kumar, BS   95

CONCLUSION   99

REFERENCES AND RECOMMENDED READINGS   101

APPENDIX   105

LIST OF FIGURES

Figure 1.1 Taxonomic Organization of Life Forms   12

Figure 1.2 Timeline of Evolution of Life on Earth   12

Figure 2.1 Drawing an elephant by connecting the dots   15

Figure 2.2 Geometric confusion   16

Figure 3.1 Children playing on a slide   23

Figure 4.1 Student reading a book without any digital distraction 42

Figure 5.1 Revised Bloom's taxonomy   52

Figure 7.1 Factors that motivate a student to do their best   75

Figure 8.1 Exercise is important to keep body and mind healthy   80

Figure 9.1 Reaching your goal takes persistent efforts   87

Introduction

During the past thirty years of teaching and conducting research at the University of Texas at Austin, I have seen several thousands of students come with dreams of becoming a medical doctor, nurse, pharmacist, engineer, scientist, or other professional. About ten years ago, I realized only 60 percent of students graduate in six years nationwide (NCES.ed.gov) and wanted to help as many students succeed as possible. If you ask any student sitting in any classroom if they ever wanted to fail that class, I don't think any hands would go up at any time. This problem of 40 percent of students not earning their degree in six years is exacerbated even more when graduates are underprepared for real life and accept underpaying jobs as they are unable to get jobs with their qualifications. Cumulatively, the nation's student debt is over $1.6 trillion at the time of writing this book, and it has become an increasing burden on students and their families. I wanted to do something to help, if even in a small way, with the hope that even if it helps just one student, it will be worth it. With this mission, I cofounded a company called "Squarecap" (graduation cap) in 2013 that focuses on helping teachers engage with their students effectively. What started with just 120 students has now been used by more than 100,000 students at over 50 universities. In 2020 I founded "Squarecap Academy" to help reach and guide students to succeed in their school work and graduate on time.

This book is another effort for the same mission, and I hope this will reach and help even more students.

I started out by studying the challenges that students face during their college days and the academic reasons for success and failure. In addition, I was also observing those successful students who strived for excellence and attained their dream jobs and were doing very well. While there is so much literature and information on this subject of student success, written by experts and researchers, the information is very spread out and scattered. It does not reach the students who are actually facing these challenges, and it cannot be found in a digestible manner in one place. This book is an attempt to summarize my observations from both students who succeeded in college and those who succumbed to the challenges and dropped out, as well as the vast amount of information gained from the science of education, psychology, cognitive neuroscience, and simple practical words of wisdom from some of my successful students.

I was born and brought up in a household of modest means in India. I went to public schools that taught their courses in the regional language, Tamil; English was only a second language we learned. The main focus of learning was memorization, but learning came naturally to me and I enjoyed all subjects, in particular biology. I do not remember a single time that I was worried about my grades or where I waited anxiously about graduating from one grade to another. I was fortunate to be admitted to one of the best agricultural universities in India where I was given the opportunity to learn and practice agricultural science. When I graduated from the Tamil Nadu Agricultural University, my father said he could not afford to send me to graduate school. I did not get upset about it but was grateful that he had given me the best education possible. I competed for, and received, a national merit scholarship from the Indian Council for Agricultural Research, and I completed my master's program with a perfect grade point average and several medals.

Even though I received a full scholarship to do my PhD in India, my ambition was always to come to the United States for my doctorate and conduct original research, but not in India. After my master's degree, I worked with the multinational corporation Monsanto Chemicals of India Ltd for three years and at Monsanto Singapore for two years, which gave me valuable field experience in product development and the corporate world. My supervisors at that time, Dr. Richard Schumacher and Dr. Russ Schneider, were instrumental in recommending me to gain admission for the PhD program at Louisiana State University, as well as three other US universities. I selected Louisiana State University, Baton Rouge because of their program; Dr. Lynn Kitchen gave me a research assistantship for my entire PhD program, with plant health as a major and biochemistry as a minor. After Dr. Kitchen left for an industry job two years into my graduate studies, I was fortunate to have Dr. Norimoto Murai as my major advisor for further research and studies in molecular biology and biochemistry.

At every stage of my education, from K-12 to graduate school to my bachelor's and master's to my PhD programs, I thoroughly enjoyed every course I ever took. I could spend countless hours in the library and loved doing research. My parents, in-laws, wife, and two children have always supported me in every step of my education. Starting with elementary school all the way up to my PhD level classes, I was there 100 percent, paying full attention, taking good notes during class, and soaking up all that the teachers were explaining. I found I did not have to study too much, except for reviewing materials before exams, but the PhD program was the hardest of all, and I had to spend extra time studying outside of class. When I started graduate school for my PhD, I read a book called *Study for Success* by Meredith Gall and Joyce Gall (1985) which helped me tremendously to excel in graduate school. This "Study for Success" book is another inspiration for writing this book, so I can help students of the current generation and future generations to come.

After completing the PhD, I did a postdoctoral fellowship at the University of Texas at Austin studying the molecular mechanisms of plants against

4

fungal disease. During this time, I had an opportunity to teach a large class on Cell and Molecular Biology to 212 students at 8 a.m. on Tuesdays and Thursdays. I had never taught a class or even worked as a teaching assistant during graduate school, but I had a blast teaching that biology course to freshmen undergraduate students. I enjoyed every bit of it and felt more energized after the class than before; I loved what I could offer to change students' lives for the better. It was a totally different satisfaction and pleasure compared to doing research which I had always thoroughly enjoyed. That teaching journey became a full-blown passion and my life-long profession, resulting in several awards from the departmental level to the state level. I still remember asking one of my best students, Mark Adkins, in that first semester of teaching in the fall of 1992 to stand up in the middle of class and share his study habits with the rest of the students to help them excel in their studies. He later did research with me on plant defense and graduated to go to Harvard University Law School. I am still in touch with Mark, and I am delighted to have an article on his educational experience in this book. Above all, I have felt the true reward of being a teacher that comes from the successes of my students as they go places and make a real change in the world. I have learned from my own children and students as much, or even more, than I have ever taught them.

In addition to sharing my personal experiences, other factors instrumental in writing this book include what I have learned from the rich literature on the science of learning and cognitive psychology and the observations and feedback shared by my successful students. I am most grateful to colleagues and past students who have written articles for this book and shared their experiences and study habits that helped them accomplish their academic dreams: Dr. Martin Perez, MD, MBA, FHM, (internal medicine); Dr. Fahmi Farah, MD (invasive cardiologist); Mr. Mark Adkins, BA, Plan II Honors and JD (Harvard Law School, corporate lawyer, and president of Muir Capital Inc.); Mr. Omar Vayani, BS Honors (currently at The University of Chicago Pritzker School of Medicine); and Mr. Sriram Palepu, BS Honors (currently at the University of Pennsylvania Perelman School of Medicine). The advice from these students who have worked hard with passion, discipline, and diligence and who have succeeded in their goals will not only inspire current students but will also provide practical tips to excel. I hope these articles will serve as role models for students aspiring to be doctors, scientists, or managers.

As I went through twenty-three years of schooling, there were many teachers who guided, inspired, and helped me find the true potential of my life. I looked at every opportunity to learn as something new; I tried to understand it to the fullest extent and apply it in real life. Education made a huge difference in transforming my life in so many ways. Starting this journey from a modest beginning with my studies at a public elementary school in a village in India, I earned a doctoral degree from a US tier 1 research university and established a teaching career at The University of Texas at Austin, one of the best universities in the nation and the world. I am fortunate to have been able to accomplish all this and be able to reflect on my life lessons to help others. I wanted to share my journey and offer more structured advice and success tips to my students to help them find their passion in life and succeed in whatever major or field they want to excel in. In addition to academic skills and mastering content knowledge, soft skills such as determination, perseverance, teamwork, steadfastness, and managing stressful situations in a positive way are also very important for ensuring academic success.

This book is organized into three units with the first unit focusing on knowledge and how to apply it by seeing the big picture and connecting the dots. The second unit focuses on study skills required to gain knowledge drawing from both cognitive science and principles of education based on research evidence. The third unit focuses on building the motivation to study, and it elaborates on both physical and mental health. I focused mainly on the academic aspects of student success and not on the social, financial, or family aspects that also impact their success in graduating from college. You can read these chapters sequentially or select a particular chapter and read what is important and relevant to your needs, interests, or situation.

Thanks so much to Sentia Publishing Company for publishing this book and the company President, William England for his patience, kind nudging, to make this happen. In addition, I am grateful to Susan Patton for copy editing and Crystal L. Kovacic of Pearl Production Inc, for helping with this publication. I hope the students will find the content of this book and suggestions to be meaningful and practically useful, and can turn them into action plans for your own success and transformation in life. Best wishes to every student for their academic success and graduation.

K. Sata Sathasivan, July 2020

Unit 1. Knowledge

It can't be stolen from its place; If bestowed, it won't diminish;

Because of its lofty stature, even an angry king can't seize it;

Legacy worth leaving for one's children is knowledge alone,

Not anything else.

Nālaṭiyār, ancient Tamil poem, ca. 3rd century

Chapter 1. Start with a Big Picture

When you visit Disney World, the first thing they hand over after you purchase the ticket is a map of the entire theme park that highlights the major attractions, how to go from one point to another point, where the restaurants and rest rooms are located, and so on. Then you can decide where to go first and how to plan the rest of your visit to cover all the aspects of the theme park. This map serves as the big picture and helps you best navigate an attraction you will visit for only a few days or maybe a week.

You subconsciously do this all the time at home or when you walk around at school; you have a big picture in your mind while navigating through the house or the campus. This sort of navigational system is intuitive and instinctive in all of us, but we often fail to see this or develop such a big picture for academic subjects. This chapter provides some examples and highlights the usefulness of the big picture habit.

When taking a semester-long course in your major, or really with education in any field, you want to start with a big picture. The big picture for your entire college program is usually given by your academic advisor when you start in a particular major. The big picture for a course is usually the syllabus that the professor distributes on the first day of class. This may be only the beginning of the semester, but you want to get organized in such a way as to master the knowledge of each chapter in the textbook assigned to you.

Knowing the big picture is similar to searching for a place on Google Maps or another similar application. The map shows you the big picture of the city where you are looking for an address, and you can zoom in or zoom out to get a perspective of where you are and where you want to go. Learning works very much like this as knowing the big picture will help you understand where you are in terms of knowledge and what you need to accomplish to get an excellent grade. Similar to directions as shown in Google Maps, you can also build a road map to accomplish your learning goals once you know the destination or learning outcome.

In the scientific world, the millions of life forms are organized in a taxonomic system starting with a big picture. Figure 1.1 shows an example of such a big picture and helps us understand the hierarchical organization and relationships of various organisms. Similarly, there has been so much knowledge accumulated in the sciences and arts over the past two centuries; it is really unprecedented in the history of humankind. Unless we see the big picture and organize the content knowledge in such a way so we can access it and understand it, we will not be able to apply it to real life.

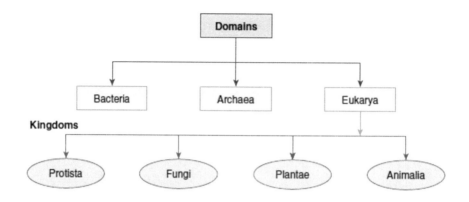

Figure 1.1. Taxonomic Organization of Life Forms

To go even further, you'll want to consider organizing each chapter of every book assigned in your courses into sub sections; note key words and how they are related to each other through concept maps or flow charts (see Chapter 5) before you begin mastering the knowledge. In the case of long chapters in English literature or US history without any subheadings, such organizations may not be very visible at the outset, but as you learn various sections of the chapter, the characters and facts emerge so you can build a big picture.

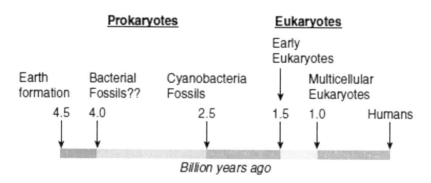

Figure 1.2. Timeline of Evolution of Life on Earth

For example, when learning a series of historical events, you may want to consider a time line chart, as shown in Figure 1.2, and expand on it with images, story lines, and brief descriptions. There are also some online programs available to help create illustrated time lines. Such big picture organization helps you in not only accessing the information but also in seeing the relationships and applying the knowledge. In addition, this helps reduce anxiety by mastering the content and developing a perspective of the learning tasks on hand so you can plan your time accordingly. While developing this big picture, if you are not sure how the system works in a particular subject, you may want to ask your professor or teaching assistants.

Getting the big picture of content knowledge is only the starting point for laying a foundation that will help you to understand the details of the content knowledge. This can be developed by reading the units of a textbook, the chapters in each unit, and the subtopics of each chapter. In some cases, prior knowledge may be helpful but is not critical. Any prior knowledge you may have can be either helpful or hindering based on the quality, depth, and accuracy of such prior knowledge. In the next chapter, we will go through this in more depth.

The practical importance of developing a big picture is very useful in taking closed book exams; in this way you can trace the facts based on the big picture organization of a chapter or topic and recall needed information and apply it to the questions you are trying to answer. It is like our daily routines; it is not so difficult to navigate a college campus when you have an approximate idea of east campus, west campus, north campus and south campus. With that big picture, you can find the classroom or building you need to go to.

Seeing the big picture helps solve problems in real life, such as understanding the human genome project, global warming, or the universe. In the modern era, big data is based on collecting vast amounts of information and then looking for patterns and the big picture so that the knowledge can be used to understand complex processes, predict outcomes, and better prepare for desirable results. While it may be hard to see the big picture when you are just starting college or completing undergraduate studies, it can be learned in a gradual manner; by paying attention to the details of every subject you are studying and thinking at a higher level, you can form a big picture of any subject or chapter. This will help you organize complex subject matter with organized subtopics to help you remember, recall, and apply. Lastly, developing the big picture also gives you a perspective on life and helps you prioritize instead of worrying about the little things that can bother you and prevent you from excelling in your studies.

Chapter 2. Connecting the Dots

While playing as a child you may have seen some coloring books with dots and numbers that you could connect with a pencil to form a figure, such as an elephant or giraffe. You can see an example of this below. The idea behind this type of activity is to help a child develop hand-eye coordination, assisting them to write and draw so they can finally see how the various dots when connected together form a new picture that was not easily visible at first.

Figure 2.1 Drawing an elephant by connecting the dots (from
http://www.supercoloring.com/dot-to-dots/elephant)

This idea of connecting the dots will gradually get more and more difficult as you learn more complex concepts where you have to make your own dots to make the big picture visible. Such analysis is done in finding patterns of development in biology, understanding causes and results in natural sciences, making sense of unrelated events in history, or building an electrical circuit in engineering.

Shown below is a diagram showing the complexity in a system expressed as connected dots seemingly done at a three-dimensional level.

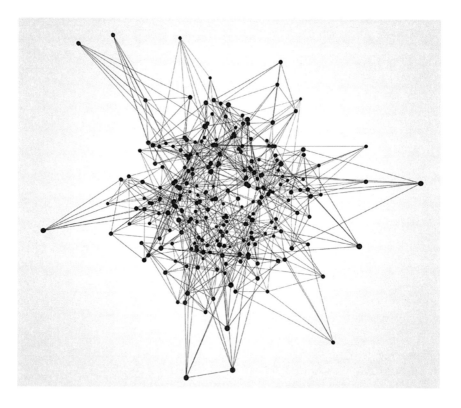

Figure 2.2. Geometric confusion
(from https://elements.envato.com/geometric-confusion-backgrounds-FS9P6T)

When you are starting to learn some basic concepts, terms, or whole sets of new information, they may seem meaningless or disconnected at first, but by carefully looking at the information or data set, you can realize a pattern is emerging. This helps you understand the given information and gain a big picture. Such approaches are commonly used in the research of complex concepts, and by doing data analysis scientists can find a pattern or a model that emerges to explain a phenomenon or process.

Many application questions found in science could be easily answered by seeing the relationships between terms, concepts, and connections. For example, consider the question 'how does salt prevent ice formation during freezing weather conditions?' To answer, you need to understand the nature of water with partial positive and negative charges, attracting to each other to form hydrogen bonds that result in ice, and the nature of salt dissociating in water resulting in Na^+ and Cl^- ions that will block the water molecules to form ice by interfering with the hydrogen bonding. This explanation is basically connecting the dots or concepts in this case to understand how the various processes and materials are connected. You may also see this logic applied to mathematical problems in which you solve the problems step by step instead of jumping to an answer. The steps in solving such math problems would be the dots that help you learn the big picture.

Why do you need to learn this, and how do you develop these skills? Basic recall of information would only help you so much in remembering and regurgitating the facts, but it will not help you in application questions in sciences and engineering or word problems in mathematics. Understanding the concepts and knowing the logical connections of the facts would help you answer such questions correctly. In addition, if you learn to apply them in one context, you could expect to apply the same in a different context. For example, related to the question on how salt prevents ice formation, think about how certain plants and animals do not freeze to death and survive even harsh winters at freezing temperatures. That would help you understand how animals have developed insulation and some plants have developed antifreeze-like chemicals and other structural adaptations.

Connecting the dots will also help you see causes and results, visualize complex patterns, and break big projects into manageable chunks to better accomplish your goals. You may have heard the story about the six blind men trying to describe an elephant. One felt its trunk and said it was like a long tubular snake and another person felt the tusk and described it like a sharp hard spear, and so on. Until you fully understand the material and realize the connections, it is hard to visualize this big picture. Sometimes not all the dots are visible, but as you learn more terms and concepts, come to understand the material better, and learn from teachers and teaching assistants, you will start to see the dots connecting to answer the questions being asked.

In many case studies of a particular social, economic, scientific, or medical issue, researchers collect all the possible information, assemble it in such a manner so the whole picture emerges, and construct a model or develop more detailed studies. There is a higher level of connecting the dots when you get involved with research, but you can always use this approach for developing an important study skill.

Chapter 3. Application is Key

Gaining an education in science, engineering, business management, journalism, film making, advertising, fine arts, liberal arts, or any other subject matter is to not only gain valuable knowledge but also to get trained in applying such concepts so that you can use your knowledge and skills to get a job and succeed in whatever you do. Application of concepts and theories comes from both complete understanding of the subject matter and practicing the application in not only attempting questions that demand application but also in doing laboratory experiments or working on real life projects. The more you practice the more you would learn to apply.

Many students approach me after completing an exam to express their difficulties and frustrations with questions related to the application of concepts. They say it is easy for them to remember and recall concepts, but they cannot apply such concepts to a given situation. For example, you can memorize the definition of moles and molarity but to make a molar solution of a certain volume needs the application of theoretical knowledge and practice to make such a solution in a laboratory. You may learn about the laws of thermodynamics but applying such laws in practical terms to biology, chemistry, or physics needs practice and more practice after you thoroughly understand the concepts of such laws.

Another example is the concept of Gibbs free energy (the energy available to do work) as in the equation shown below:

$$\Delta G = \Delta H - T \Delta S$$

The ΔG refers to the net change in free energy, ΔH refers to the net change in enthalpy or potential energy, T is absolute temperature in Kelvin, and ΔS refers to the net change in entropy or the measure of randomness.

For a reaction to be spontaneous or favorable, the net change in free energy (ΔG) needs to be negative, meaning there is a net loss or release of free energy. Such concepts may be initially hard to grasp, but with proper examples you may understand such concepts and be able to apply them in real life. Examples of such spontaneous reactions are melting ice at room temperature, burning fossil fuels to release energy in the form of heat, and evaporation of water at high temperatures. Fossil fuels store energy, and after they are burned, they have less energy and hence a loss of free energy. By using these examples and understanding the concepts, one can apply the concept of free energy and then answer any question that is not related to any of these examples. We will see how you can apply this concept to a different context of children playing on a slide.

Figure 3.1. Children playing on a slide.

The child standing at the top of the slide has relatively more potential and free energy than the child standing on the ground. So, based on this, you can infer when the child sliding from the top to the bottom of the slide is losing potential and free energy as they are going from a high to a low position. This is a qualitative way of applying this free energy concept, but there are also actual numbers for the enthalpy, absolute temperature, and entropy that you can enter in the free energy equation and figure out the answer. Thus, to apply the theoretical knowledge you need to understand the concepts first, learn some examples of various types of such processes, and then practice them with either qualitative or quantitative information.

Other types of applications come from practically doing experiments, projects, and internships or volunteering. Many laboratory skills and physical skills such as swimming or canoeing do not come from simply reading the materials or watching a video about such sports but from practicing them regularly and intentionally. Another technique that will help develop application skills is model building. You may learn about how to build a bridge in a civil engineering class, but unless you practically build one, such knowledge may not be useful. However, you cannot build a real bridge right away but must develop practice by building a model bridge on a miniature scale by applying all the engineering principles that you learned. Only when you practice such skills in a safe and proper manner can you improve and succeed in such areas. Hence look for courses that offer you not only theory but also practice in what you are learning. Pay attention to learning the terms and concepts and seek opportunities to do practice problems or perform skills that need physical activities.

Conducting research is another way to learn practical skills and apply theoretical knowledge. However, as an undergraduate student, it may be hard to find professors or labs that will admit undergraduates. Fortunately, there are structured undergraduate research programs, such as the Freshmen Research Initiative (FRI) at The University of Texas at Austin and similar programs, that have expanded nationwide using this model. However, doing research may not be for everyone as it comes with its own risks and rewards. First of all, before conducting research one must learn the safety rules and practical skills necessary to operate equipment or use a chemical. The rewards of research are manyfold in not only experiencing the discovery, innovation, and invention first-hand and exploring the scientific frontiers but also in giving you the opportunity to possibly publish research papers as a first or coauthor. This lays a great foundation for graduate school or professional school.

Finding internships or volunteering opportunities are other ways of developing practical application skills necessary to explore various interests and narrowing down which path you want to take for the rest of your time in college or in life. There are many student organizations that foster such volunteering opportunities, as well as structured programs in colleges and departments, local hospitals, non-profit organizations off campus, and some national level organizations that you can find on the internet. Your professors and teaching assistants are also valuable resources to explore research opportunities. Such volunteering opportunities will provide a valuable experience and may lead to a paying job or pave the way to specializing in college and beyond. They also can screen out the areas that you do not enjoy so you may not consider them again.

Lastly, do not be afraid of failure in applying a theory to practice and in conducting research because that is the nature of real-life experience and research. But learn from every failure and mistake and improve your performance over time. And also pay full attention to safety rules and follow them for not only your personal safety but also for the safety of others.

Personal Success Story 1

Dr. Martin Perez, MD, MBA, FHM

President, Founder, House Physicians Texas

I consider myself self-motivated but having three siblings go to college before me made my decision to succeed academically much easier. In addition, my parents both had college degrees, so I knew how important education was to them. They never told me that I had to pursue any specific degree or profession, but I knew they wanted me to do my best. I was taught that deep knowledge could open many doors and create job opportunities. When I was in high school, I knew early on that effort and discipline were critical to academic success. In any subject, good outcomes come from excellent time management and focus. You need to first define what academic success means to you and why. I believe academic success is gaining the essential knowledge to achieve a higher personal or professional goal that allows you to compete at the highest level. You need to be relentless and determined in your efforts. You also need to turn mistakes and failures into opportunities for growth and learning.

Although I did not know exactly what I wanted to be when I was a teenager, I knew that I loved science. While in high school, I had to develop good study habits on a regular basis. I reinforced the good habits and stopped the bad ones. Although I initially thought that homework was sometimes "busy work," I realized that it was mainly for reinforcement of daily lessons. Time management, prioritization of tasks, and focused effort saved me valuable time in an otherwise short and chaotic high school day. Preparing for tests such as the ACT and SAT is crucial to understanding the format and the time allotted to take them. I also recommend taking an honors course and participating in an extracurricular activity to understand time management. You must remember that college entrance is based on your patterns of preparedness and successes. In addition, you cannot forget that strong reading and writing skills play a vital role in your academic success. Academic success is not just an excellent grade but the result of persistent application.

After getting accepted into college as a microbiology major, I realized that the course work was much heavier and detailed. I also knew that I had to be dedicated and more organized since class attendance was not always mandatory. You typically will not have anyone in college to tell you to wake up, go to school, or even to study. You need to rely on self-motivation and study groups to keep yourself engaged in the subject matter. I keep mentioning "self-motivation" because no matter how many times people tell you how to be successful, you are the only one who will make it happen. Anything worth having will not come easy. You need to write down your academic and personal tasks and prioritize them by deadline and level of difficulty. My professors were dedicated, but they were not there to tell me when and how to be successful. Their job was to teach the course, and my job was to learn as much as possible so that I could do well on the exams and assignments. Again, great effort and time management result in good grades.

In addition, do not forget that books, tuition fees, and housing are all part of the whole equation. Everyone's financial situation is different in college, and it can make an impact on your grades if you need to balance a job and school. I paid for most of my college expenses with scholarships, part-time jobs, and college work-study programs. I was fortunate to be in a work-study program in a science department that not only paid me for my work but also allowed me to work with a professor who became my mentor. My mentor inspired me to pursue my education past college. I refined my definition of academic success by emulating those who were already academically successful. My work-study paved the way and opened doors to my post-graduate education. In the last year of college, I wanted to pursue a career in medicine and become a physician. Getting into medical school required that I study efficiently for the Medical College Admission Test (MCAT). I had several study partners who were also motivated to enter medical school. It is important to surround yourself with others who are motivating and motivated.

After being accepted into medical school, I learned that you need to study more effectively since there is so much more information to learn in a short time. I recommend reviewing the lecture materials before going to the lecture as you are likely to retain more and ask thoughtful questions. Avoid getting overwhelmed by details and ask for help from fellow students and professors when a concept does not make sense. Understand key concept and high-yield facts. Do not be overwhelmed by all the course material as you cannot learn everything. The first two years of medical school can be tremendously rigorous by the sheer volume of information, so never give up. You might have to shift gears and adjust your study habits to fit the new material and schedule. The first two years of medical school are mostly theory, so the best way to retain important information is by reinforcement and repetition. The third and fourth years of medical school are mostly practical, and you will finally be able to see your theory in action while taking care of patients. I believe that both theory and practice are critical in reinforcing knowledge throughout your career. While in medical school, you will also start preparing for the medical licensing exam (USMLE), so recollection of key principles and concepts is essential.

In conclusion, even after your education is considered "done," you are just beginning a new and exciting journey to academic success. I study more efficiently now and read daily just to stay updated on the constant flow of new information. Avoid getting overwhelmed, stay organized, maintain your habits, and keep your mind and body healthy. Find which study habits give you the best outcomes and the best balance in your life. Do not forget that academic success comes from effort and enthusiasm. Find your definition of success and pursue it relentlessly, and do not withdraw when failures or mistakes hit you at times. Keep learning and growing as this is all part of academic success.

Personal Success Story 2

Mark Adkins, BA, University of Texas at Austin, Plan II Honors

JD, Harvard Law School. President, Muir Capital Inc.

I can still remember the moment when I decided to go from being a "good" student to being a "great" student. It was in the summer after my freshman year in high school. I was sitting in the backyard reading a magazine article about science. I suddenly realized that I was fascinated with the subject matter. I can remember thinking: "*I really enjoy learning.*" From that moment, through the rest of high school, through earning perfect grades in an Honors Program at the University of Texas, through applying for and being admitted to the best law schools in the country (including Stanford, Columbia, and about a dozen others), and ultimately earning a J.D. from Harvard Law School, I never again accepted simply coasting through my schooling.

I had not been a terrible student as a freshman in high school, but I had yet to tap into my true potential. I was just going through the motions, without a clear plan or objective. When I returned to high school as a sophomore, I decided to take my summer's realization of "I enjoy learning!" and apply it to every course. I paid attention in each class and focused on taking detailed class notes. I read the material and then, critically, learned the all-important lesson that repetition of the teacher's course material is the key to mastery. When my first tests came back with high grades, I enjoyed earning them so much that I wanted to do it again. I started applying myself more and more with each passing semester. I remember talking to a friend who asked me, "why do you care so much about the course?" I was struck off guard by this, and thought, "because I want to do well!" I never stopped having that desire to do well and became better and better at studying.

At the outset of my freshman year at the University of Texas in the Plan II Honors Program, I deliberately told myself, "don't repeat your mistakes of high school, where you didn't start off with your best foot forward." I reminded myself, "instead try your very best from the beginning of the first year." I made straight 'A's in the first semester, then again in the next, and again and again. Overall, I did not stress too much about grades because I enjoyed my classes and the process of learning. The only time I felt intense pressure to earn 'A's was in my final semester as a senior, when I did not want to lose a perfect GPA. That was the first time I felt like I was trying to take the class just to earn a good grade instead of wanting to master the course.

This drive, or desire, to learn and succeed academically that started for me in my summertime backyard after my freshman year in high school, and continued on through college and law

32

school, is to me the first and foremost ingredient of several core ingredients to academic success. A second is having a clear objective, or goal, or as Dr. Sata would say, "road map." The third is repetition (also known as hard work).

The coursework in college, of course, was much more challenging than in high school, but the fundamental academic skillsets required for success were the same. Dr. Sata emphasizes that a student must have a "road map" in the holistic sense of understanding their goals and objectives and what steps are necessary to achieve them. I learned quickly that this need for a road map applies not only in the grand sense of having an academic mission (or goal) for one's undergraduate experience but also a road map for success in each particular course. Indeed, this road map is usually immediately discerned in the course syllabus. But in greater detail, it is virtually always given in the professor's course lecture. In school, as in life, there is vastly more information than any one of us can possibly master. Yet we can master, and become expert at, specific pieces of information. Succeeding in a course requires mastering not all information but the specific information prioritized by the course. The professor is both our guide as a well as our judge. The successful student, therefore, focuses and prioritizes on the specific information that the professor emphasizes. For example, in my first year of college I took a course on the history of Great Britain. Wanting to master all the information, I took it upon myself to get a second book on British history, not part of the curriculum. For the first test, I studied the course material, but I also studied this additional book on the same period. That exam was my worst performance in the course. I was so disappointed not to have done better on the first exam, despite having gone what I thought was an "extra mile," so I met with the professor and asked for advice on how to improve. She immediately pointed out that my mistake was to spend precious study time on material that was not in the curriculum. In other words, that was not on the road map. From then on, I focused my efforts on studying the class lecture notes. I would read the textbook as background, but I would study, over and over, the course notes. Repetition, again and again, was critical to fully and deeply understanding the material. In this course, the exams were timed written essays. Mastery of the information, to be used effectively, must be prioritized. By focusing and fully mastering the course lecture material, I was completely prepared for any essay question because I could articulate the information most important to the course. Additional information, in fact, would simply distract.

Repetition worked for me whether it was a math course, chemistry, history, English, or, of course, a biology course with Dr. Sata. Reading and rereading the lecture notes, doing and redoing the math or science questions, or, in the case of an English literature course, reading and rereading the subject books or works, always was the key to mastery of the professor's course material. In the case of advanced math courses, I found that doing the course problems over and over always prepared me for the exam material and led me to master the subject matter. In the case of essays, I found that writing and re-writing was critical. After studying the material, I would come up with my core concept and then try to get a first draft on paper. If I got stuck, I would go on long walks thinking through the material. Somehow, the walking would loosen up the ideas in my head and let them start to flow. But getting the first draft was just the beginning. Editing and re-editing, repeatedly, was critical. My understanding of the material would evolve in the process of writing and rewriting. Thoughts would crystalize. Insights would develop. Over time, my language would improve. But again, repetition must be focused—focused on the prioritized road map provided by the professor.

On the holistic level, the effectiveness of repetition is equally clear. I was happy that I had applied for the Plan II Honors Program at the University of Texas and been admitted, but in my heart, I felt that my approach in high school to applying for and being admitted to colleges was haphazard and unfocused. During my application process to post graduate school, I wanted to be deliberate and effective in my process. The ingredients are easily apparent again: first, the principal ingredient of desire and drive. It can come from that first realization of how fun it is to learn or from a desire to succeed, but it must come from within. Second, the goal, or objective, or road map. Here, my goal became going to law school and then, even more clearly, to getting into Harvard Law School in particular. Third, the all-important concept of applied hard work. I set about learning the fundamental elements needed to get accepted to the program. Just as the professor's course syllabus and lectures are the road map to course success, understanding the goals of the law school admission board become critical to succeeding in getting admitted. I met with law school alumni and read about applying for law school. Unlike in high school, when I focused on my class work and viewed the SAT as an "add-on," I prepared for the LSAT as if it were another course. Taking prep courses and, of course, practicing my time-honored concept of "repetition," I took and retook practice exams. I applied for internship programs and was accepted to a State Department internship at the U.S. Embassy in Panama. This program provided me key life experiences which formed the underpinnings of my essays for law school. I knew that law school admissions programs wanted to admit students who would succeed in their school and who would also become successful alumni. They wanted to see outstanding grades, great LSAT scores, and interesting life experiences that showed a drive to achieve. None of these things, of course, just occur. They are all the product of focused and dedicated effort aimed at achieving a specific objective.

During our long academic career as students, we encounter countless teachers, lecturers and professors. Almost all of them, certainly all the best of them, are obsessed with their subject matter. If they teach constitutional history, they love to study, research, and write about constitutional history. If they teach chemistry, they love to research and experiment in chemistry. In Dr. Sata's case, it's teaching biology, and he loves to conduct research and passionately study plant chromosomes and NADPH Cytochrome P450 Reductase. But what is unique, and unusual, for students to encounter in their academic career are teachers or professors who not only love their subject matter but also, and here is the special part, teaching their students and ensuring their success. Sadly, very few professors view it as their job or their business, really, to think about the holistic success of their students. Dr. Sata is that exceptional professor. He has made it his career to contribute to the knowledge base of biology through his research and study but, also, to enhance and improve the overall academic success of his students.

Unit 2. Study Skills

Anyone who stops learning is old, whether at twenty or eighty. Anyone who keeps learning stays young. The greatest thing in life is to keep your mind young.

Henry Ford

Chapter 4. Art of Memorization

Learning any new subject includes knowing new terms, facts, concepts, and applications in that subject. When I was an undergraduate, about forty-six years ago, life was simple and the overall content of each subject was very limited. But now with the explosion of information, the content covered in each course is vast, deep, and detailed. For example, I remember one biochemistry textbook from graduate school, by Stryer, was 1064 pages long while my undergraduate notes (no textbooks at that time) were barely 100 pages long. Hence surface level, casual reading of the material is not sufficient to do well in college level courses nowadays.

I have students come into my office concerned about their grades who say, "Dr. Sata, I love biology but I don't know how to study biology and do well in the exams." I ask them about their prior knowledge of biology, why they are taking the course and how they study for exams. Then I go through their past exams to help them understand why they missed some of the questions and how they can improve their study skills. There are systematic ways of learning vast amounts of information in a short time, and there are ways to improve your exam scores.

The whole process of effectively learning vast amounts of information can be summarized in the four Rs:

1. **Read the textbook and assigned materials:** Reading the textbook and assignment materials before you go to class and after you attend the class is essential. While reading the textbook, browse the entire chapter and see how it is organized and how it relates to the unit within the book. That gives you a context to focus on regarding specific contents of the topic you are about to read. Glance through the text and then go through any figures. Stop highlighting or underlining key words since you will end up highlighting more sections than you want, and it is a passive way of learning. Your brain will tune out after paying attention to some parts of the highlighted material. Instead write down the key words and their definitions in your own words (see Step 4 below) and make an outline. Keep any digital distractions, such as cell phone and TV, off while reading serious textbooks. When you read for the first time, try more to understand the content than to memorize; try to find the context and connections, and try to see the big picture or how this information fits into it.

2. **Reflect on what you read:** Reading the same content repeatedly is not as effective as read-reflect-read-reflect-read and so on. This gives you time to think about what you have read and process the content for better understanding. Make note of the content that was not clear to you. Reading without any reflection assumes that you have understood what you have read or delays the understanding of what you are reading. Try to reach out to the professor or teaching assistant to seek help during the

class or office hours or by email to understand anything that did not make sense to you.

Figure 4.1. Student reading a book without any digital distraction

3. **Rephrase and organize:** After you have completed the read-reflect-read again on a particular topic or subtopic, write down the key terms and concepts and outline the material in your own words without copying the textbook verbatim. This type of processing information and rephrasing it is part of learning. Organize the content in such a way that you can use them to remember and practice recall. You can organize the content as a list, outline, concept map, flow chart, table, Venn diagram, or figure. See the next chapter for various examples of such. Keep them organized and avoid compiling them in a confusing way, such as mind mapping which is not hierarchical with connections that can go in multiple ways unless that is the only way to connect various aspects of

the content. Also, when you are organizing them into flash cards or tables, write them in such a way as to practice recall by hiding one part of the paper or one side of the flash card when you are trying to memorize them.

4. **Retrieval/recall practice:** The last step in remembering is to test yourself to see if you can recall the information. You could use flash cards or a table with two columns that you can use similar to flash cards by hiding one section of the table and trying to remember the meaning of the term. If you use flash cards, try to keep them organized so that you don't confuse words that are similar but have a totally different meaning. Self-quiz tools from the textbook or outside sources could also be used to practice recall. You can also use online tools such as Quizlet to practice your own quizzes or the quizzes made by others. You may also ask your professor for practice questions or sample exam questions to practice recall. This is a very important step in remembering because such skill is essential in doing well on exams. This is as important as someone learning violin or practicing a competitive sport such as basketball or football.

There are also some shortcuts to remembering facts and concepts, such as mnemonics and acronyms. Mnemonics refers to memory in Greek, and you can arrange difficult to remember facts, such as organizing the taxonomic classification system of Kingdom, Phylum, Class, Order, Family, Genus, Species, with the mnemonics, "**K**ing **P**layed

Chess On Fine Grain Sand." You may be familiar with the mnemonics to remember the eight planets in the solar system: Mercury, Venus, Earth, Mars, Jupitar, Saturn, Uranus and Neptune with the phrase "**M**y **V**ery **E**legant **M**other **J**ust **S**howed **U**p **N**icely." Feel free to make up your own mnemonics to remember a set of terms that are not logically connected.

There are other ways to practice recitals by repeating them, but these could be more effective if you understand the logic and concept behind what you are remembering. Homer's *Odyssey* was written in the 8th century in 12,000 lines; it was passed on simply by oral tradition and only later was it written down. Many ancient poems and epics of India such as Ramayana (24,000 verses) and Mahabharata (24,000 verses) are considered to be from about the 10th century BCE. They were remembered by simple recital and were passed on from generation to generation, even before any written forms existed. All these forms of memorization are time consuming, and there was a pattern to remembering such epics. That is not what you are aiming for, but you could use some aspect of memorization by recital or practice as it would apply to certain subjects such as poetry, music, singing, or performing arts.

There are some myths that prevailed for over thirty years about different people having different learning styles, such as VARK (Visual, Auditory, Reading/ writing, and Kinesthetic) styles of learning. There is no scientific evidence to support this, and it was debunked recently in 2009 by a group of psychologists.

It is obvious that we all use our senses and skills of seeing, hearing, reading, writing, and doing things. The positive outcome is that each style reinforces others to improve your learning. For example, you can learn about a new concept by seeing an image, reading about it, and watching a video on the same topic. Each of these resources complements each other and enhances overall learning. For example, one technique for memorization, such as reading out loud, reinforces seeing and hearing. Watching a video lecture by your professor or an animation about a process and taking notes includes visual and writing.

In addition, there are ways to remember things in an associative recall where you remember one thing and the related things follow as a trail of thoughts. For example, when you hear the word leaf, you can easily recall the words green, chlorophyll, and photosynthesis. Another example is when you think of the word building and related words such as brick, concrete, wood, air conditioning, and many more come to your mind. Whenever you are studying in groups it helps to quiz each other to practice recall. Teaching another person about the subject matter also helps you learn better, but if group study is not effective for you time wise, or you don't gain anything more than from studying alone, it is just fine to learn on your own. If you'd like to learn more, there is a good book called *Make It Stick: The Science of Successful Learning* by

Peter Brown, Henry Roediger III, and Mark McDaniel published in 2014. It is listed in the suggested further readings.

Chapter 5. Mechanisms of Learning

In the previous chapter, various methods for memorization were emphasized, but that is only a part or a beginning of the learning process. This chapter includes principles of learning and some more techniques to consider to study effectively.

There are so many books written on the mechanisms of learning, and one of the most recent ones, published in 2020, is *How We Learn* by Stanislas Dehaene. He is a professor of experimental cognitive psychology at the College de France and director of the Neurospin Brain Imaging Center. Dehaene has done numerous research studies and analyzed what activities and biological processes contribute to effective learning and has organized them as the four pillars of learning. Here is a brief summary of his findings; for more information, refer to his book listed as one of the recommended readings.

The four pillars of learning include attention, active engagement, error feedback, and consolidation of memory. I have added some examples and expanded on each aspect of the four pillars of learning.

1. **Attention:** The learning process starts with paying attention to what you want to learn. This includes attending all the classes and not missing any unless you have a valid health issue or another reason. I have seen many students start attending class for the first half of the semester and then realize that they have figured out the tricks to make an A so they stop coming to class. At the

beginning of each semester, I bring up the analogy of buying a movie ticket online. I ask the students, 'if you pay $12 for a movie ticket online have you ever then missed going to that movie?' No one says they missed or forgot to go to the movie. Then I ask them, 'do you know how much it costs you to attend each lecture?' Some will know the answer or simply say, 'a lot.' Exactly, that is the point. Each student pays anywhere from $25 to $100 per hour of instruction depending on whether it is in-state fees at a public university or out-of-state fees at a private ivy league university. If you are paying that much money for each hour of lecture, why would you miss it? Showing up is almost 80 percent of the task accomplished. Once you are in class, you need to pay attention to what the professor says, keeping up the attention level, and then processing the information. This is an opportunity to clarify the questions you have from your assigned readings and anything that you did not understand from that day's lecture.

2. **Engagement:** If you are physically in a classroom but your mind is wandering elsewhere, it is not going to benefit you or the professor as you could be losing all the new information being delivered and also be a source of distraction to the professor. You need to be actively listening in, thinking about it, and taking notes. Be curious to learn the subject matter and develop some interest to learn new things. Such excitement of learning will stimulate dopamine, one of the neurotransmitters for a positive feeling. You may not understand all the material

the professor is talking about, but if you pay attention, you can make a note of things that do not make sense to you and ask the professor either during pauses in the class or after the class during office hours. Try to recognize the gap between what you already know, what you are learning, and what is still not clear to you. This is like being aware of your awareness or cognition over cognition. This type of active engagement is an essential part of learning whether you are listening to a class or a seminar or reading a book. Not all subjects and professors may be interesting or engaging, but that is their nature and style of teaching. Some professors use a classroom response system to keep you engaged and participating in class discussions. Some professors will be simply lecturing for the entire class. You need to develop or have innate interest or curiosity to learn new material. It also helps to develop patience and persistence to keep learning without getting frustrated.

3. **Error feedback:** It is essential, in order for the learning process to succeed, to get quick and accurate feedback as to what was wrong in your answers or thinking and why they were wrong. This could also be done with the classroom response system during the class or flash cards, self-quizzes, and home work after the class. Making mistakes while learning new material is common, but learning from the mistakes is important to be a successful student. This aspect of learning is also emphasized by Burger and Starbird (2012) as failing to succeed. It is important that we learn from the mistakes and improvise our responses and not feel that we are being punished for

making mistakes. Trying this in self quizzes and other no-stake or low-stake assignments helps you become better in recognizing the mistakes and succeeding.

4. **Consolidation:** This is the end result of how we can master new material after paying attention, being engaged with the material, and getting feedback on our errors. This process culminates in consolidating the memory, and it happens even when we are sleeping. Sleep is an essential activity as it is when the brain recalls the events that happened prior to sleep and consolidates them to make memories. As you have no doubt experienced, lack of sleep leads to tiredness, lack of focus, inability to think critically, and overall poor learning. Fortunately, there is some flexibility in our brains called neuroplasticity that means the connections can be reformed and improved. Having a regular habit of good diet, exercise, and sufficient sleep improves your overall functioning and effectiveness.

There is another book, *Understanding How We Learn*, by Yana Weinstein and Megan Sumeracki with Oliver Caviglioli that was published in 2019 and covers the cognitive aspects of learning, incorporating all the recent findings on the learning process. The authors emphasize planning to study the subject in a spaced manner throughout the semester, elaborating on what you study each day, making connections between multiple ideas, thinking about examples, trying multiple modes of learning using texts and visuals, and practicing retrieval of what you have studied. This book gives details of how you can execute this plan with nice visuals throughout. However, the authors also emphasize not to believe in myths such as the VARK model (Visual, Auditory, Reading/writing and Kinesthetic) or the left brain/right brain concept which have both been debunked. This is also one of the suggested readings given at the end of this book.

Learning is more than memorization and retrieval practice with remembering and regurgitating. One should also learn to think effectively. Edward Burger and Michael Starbird (2012) clearly outline this in their book *The 5 Elements of Effective Thinking*. This includes five strong ideas: learning simple things deeply by paying attention to details; not being afraid to make mistakes but learning from them; asking the right questions about what you have learned and keep improving the questions; seeing the flow of ideas from the past to the future and connecting the dots; and being the change to transform yourself and to transform others. The process is an iterative process, and it works well whether you are a student just starting out or a senior scientist. This is another recommended reading listed at the end of this book.

Bloom's Taxonomy: Any discussion on learning is incomplete without covering the topic of Bloom's Taxonomy. In 1956, Benjamin Bloom, along with collaborators Max Englehart, Edward Furst, Walter Hill, and David Krathwohl, published the *Taxonomy of Educational Objectives*. It is popularly known as "Bloom's Taxonomy" among educators but not many students are familiar with this concept even though it deeply affects how they learn, take exams, understand their performance, and improve their test scores. The original Bloom's Taxonomy included Knowledge →

Comprehension → Application → Analysis → Synthesis → Evaluation; the updated framework of learning is illustrated below.

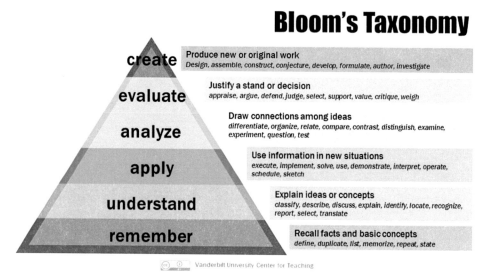

Figure 5.1 Revised Bloom's taxonomy from the Vanderbilt Center for Teaching. (via Creative Commons license)
https://cft.vanderbilt.edu/guides-sub-pages/blooms-taxonomy/

The revised taxonomy includes the steps of learning starting with remembering (recalling, facts, terms), then understanding (concepts, interpretation, classification and description), applying (to a given situation to solve problems), analyzing (organize, differentiate, compare and contrast), evaluating (critique, judge, appraise), and then creating original work that did not exist before.

As a student, one should be able to recognize a given learning outcome and the test questions within this framework of remember, understand, apply, analyze, evaluate, and create and prepare to learn accordingly and succeed.

Mary Forehand (2005) of the University of Georgia grouped knowledge into various levels such as factual knowledge (terms and facts), conceptual knowledge (theories, models, principles), procedural knowledge (skills and techniques of specific subjects), and metacognitive knowledge (context, strategic, self-knowledge). This set of knowledge can overlap with the Bloom's Taxonomy framework. For further information, refer to the article by Forehand (2005) listed in the references.

As a student you can use these research findings on learning and education in its broad sense to get the most out of your college education. It will also help you improve scores after you see exam results and go through exam wrappers (sample is provided at the end of this book) to analyze why you missed a particular question and how to improve. For example, you may notice all the questions you missed were at the mid or higher levels of Bloom's Taxonomy meaning you have no problems in remembering but need more practice in application or evaluation, etc. Also, remember the Bloom's levels are hierarchical, and knowledge is essential to understand and understanding is important to apply. Hence try to work at all levels and understand the nature of each course's expectations as some professors teach for recall but may ask application level questions and vice versa. Most professors usually test on what they teach, and they don't teach for the test, unlike high school AP courses. Be aware of the expectations of each professor, and try to get a copy of the sample exams if available. You can use the table of action verbs in Bloom's Taxonomy, given at the end of this book, to understand the nature of the question. It is perfectly fine to try out different methods and see which one works the best for you, but learn it quickly as you start college because your grades and future depends on it.

Chapter 6. Seven Principles of Smart Learning

There is a classic book, *How Learning Works: 7 Research Based Principles of Smart Teaching*, that was published in 2010 by Susan Ambrose, Michael Bridges, Michelle DiPietro, Marsha Lovett, and Marie Norman. Most of the authors are either from or associated with Carnegie Mellon University in Pittsburgh. This book and similar ones were written with teachers, educators, graduate students, faculty developers, and instructional designers as their main audiences. According to the authors of this book, these seven principles were developed based on research in cognitive development, social psychology, anthropology, education, and diversity studies of both K-12 and higher education students. I am summarizing them for the benefit of students who are the primary audience of this book and adding my own reflections on how these seven principles will strengthen your learning and success. This will also help you make the best use of the resources given by the professors.

1. **Prior knowledge:** A few students have visited my office after seeing their performance in the exams and said "I took an AP (Advanced Placement) Biology course in high school and still I am struggling in your course, what should I do?" I tell these students that "this is not an AP biology course, and this is not high school. Look around you, welcome to college!" Ambrose et al (2010) note that prior knowledge can help or hinder learning depending on if it was accurate, appropriate, sufficient, and activated. As you can see from the above example of students coming to college after completing AP biology or other courses, they expect or

assume that the course was sufficient and accurate for doing well in college courses. While this could be true and helpful, the focus, depth, and details of courses covered in colleges and universities are significantly greater than what is covered in AP courses, which are mostly exam driven. College courses are designed to teach the fundamentals for life, go deeper in every aspect of the course, and expect that students will apply what they are learning more than simple memorization. Sometimes, they have studied similar materials but the knowledge is not active anymore, and sometimes, the information they learned could be inaccurate. Another aspect of utilizing this prior knowledge is to know what one knows and does not know. Taking an inventory of terms and concepts one already knows at the expected level and then marking the terms and concepts one does not yet know well would be a good starting point. With this list students can learn further at the college level.

2. **Organizing knowledge:** As we discussed in the previous chapter, rephrasing and organizing what you have learned after reading a particular topic or chapter is important in helping you retrieve and apply such knowledge. Experts have systematic ways of organizing knowledge in simple ways, such as concept maps (Chapters 1 and 4), flow charts, and tables and figures with sufficient details. They incorporate the association of terms and concepts with each other in such summary diagrams. When you are learning new material for the first time, you may not realize the relationships and hierarchy of facts and concepts, but

as you learn more and more and process the information learned, the connections become obvious. Also, understanding the logic of how structures are related to their functions, the sequence of events that happens to complete a process, the historical timeline in a scientific discovery, and comparing and contrasting related structures or processes to know the bottom line of how deep you need to learn will help you tremendously when organizing the content that you are learning.

3. **Motivation:** Personal motivation to learn new material is very critical in deciding how much time and effort a student will dedicate to learning a particular subject. Some aspects of learning are external and some are internal, under the student's control. The external factors include teachers' expectations, how hard or difficult the course is, if the student gets a good grade if they do what the teacher expects, if the course provides any value to the student, and so on. The internal factors that affect motivation depend on the student's goals (major with interest or just a degree requirement), the values the student places on the course (covered in more detail in the chapter on motivation), and the context of the environment such as personal health, family issues, economics, and the support system at the institution. Based on surveys of my introductory biology students, it became obvious the top motivation for students is grades, followed in second place by professors who cared about teaching. Third place went to learning new materials and fourth was getting into medical/graduate school, with the last being parents. The third and fourth places were very close. Each student has

a reason to be motivated, and the academic culture has conditioned students for decades to be focused on grades and the teachers who made a difference in everyone's life, including mine. Find your source of motivation and succeed in each course.

4. **Developing mastery:** Mastering a particular subject takes time and effort. According to Ambrose et al. (2010), the three steps in mastering a particular subject are acquiring the component skills, practicing the integration skills, and learning when to apply the skills. A good analogy used by the authors is learning to drive; it requires you to know how to use the accelerator, brakes, steering wheel, and gear shift. Integration would refer to using the accelerator, brakes, and steering wheel simultaneously to drive the car safely, stay in your lane, keep track of other vehicles, and coordinate all these skills. Application will come with driving under various conditions of rain, traffic, and icy roads while still driving safely and using all the integration skills. Similarly, you can master a science course such as biology, chemistry, or physics by learning the basic laws that govern the natural world, the terms and concepts, and then integrating the various aspects of such knowledge to solve an application problem that you have not seen before. Such mastery takes time to develop, and simple cramming of the material will not work well.

5. **Practice and feedback:** Mastery of content is possible after regular practice of what you have learned and getting appropriate feedback from teachers to learn what you have missed and how you can improve. By paying attention to

the learning outcomes, the instructions of the professor, and a rubric if there is one, students can complete an assignment and try to get feedback during the preparation and after the submission has been graded. The students may get feedback from peers or teaching assistants prior to submission to make sure they have covered all aspects of a teacher's expectations. Most teachers will give specific feedback to each student, but in large classes the feedback may be group feedback. Even if some teachers do not give any feedback, you may want to approach them as to why points were taken off and see if you can receive any qualitative feedback. As we have seen before in the previous chapter on the mechanisms of learning, error feedback is an important pillar of learning (Dehaene, 2020). Practicing self-quizzes built with error feedback would also be helpful before taking high-stake exams. Seek every opportunity to learn from your mistakes.

6. **Student development and course environment:** This brings up the sensitive topics of gender bias, minority vs majority, stereotyping, sexual orientation, religious beliefs, and ethnicity bias in classroom surroundings as well as the level of maturation the students and teachers have developed to foster a conducive environment for all students to succeed in a fair and equitable manner. While all teachers are professionally trained to treat all students equally, some students may feel they are alienated or get offended when the teacher talks about such issues in class and feel very uncomfortable in dealing with it as a subject matter or as a perceived issue. In either case, it is good to meet with your teacher during office hours and share your

concern of how you or other students felt on that topic and try to correct the situation to provide the best opportunity for all students to learn and succeed. It is also important to develop a sense of belonging in every college or university that you attend, and find the support system—whether a faculty mentor, student organization, student services office, dean of student's office, or ombudsman—who can objectively analyze the issue and help rectify it if there are issues. Academic institutions should not be a place for such social discrimination on any basis.

7. **Self-directed learning:** Lastly, what promotes a life-long learner is developing a strategy to become a self-directed learner. This involves assessing the task at hand, whether it is an exam, research paper, or presentation, evaluating one's own strengths and weaknesses on that particular subject matter, developing a plan of action, and executing it. Once executed, reflect on the performance to reiterate and improve the plans and performance in a consistent and continuous basis. If the teacher has provided a list of learning outcomes or a guideline for presentation or a group project, try to understand the details; ask questions on anything that is not clear and then evaluate your strengths and weaknesses before developing a plan of action. When in doubt, ask the teacher to clarify the expectations. Incorporate any suggestions based on your own reflection or feedback from student peers.

These seven principles provide a structured way to master course content and provide a framework for understanding if you are facing any difficulties in your studies and how you can solve such problems. As additional help, understand and use the metacognitive study cycle found in the appendix.

Personal Success Story 3

Dr. Fahmi Farah, MD. Invasive Cardiologist and CEO,

Bentley Heart Director, Global Health Alliance Foundation, USA

We all have our own challenges in life and sometimes it's easy to get lost in the struggle and chaos of everyday living. Sometimes it's important for us to pause for a moment, try to zoom out of the everyday, and realize where we are to remember where we once were and focus on where we want to go from here.

As I finish another busy clinic and begin my preparation for a global webinar to discuss the current global health issues in the middle of a pandemic with some of the world leaders from the United Nations, World Health Organization, and UNICEF, I pause for a moment to think how did I get here and what was life like before this? As I look back, it's hard to imagine how many sacrifices it took and how many times I heard the word "NO" in my life. My mind went back eighteen years to 2002, the year I started college. I was so excited as I was finishing off high school to start the next chapter of my life: college. My lifelong dream was to become a doctor, and I had fantasized about going away to college for years, and it was all finally about to happen. Life was good.

Fate though had a slightly different plan for me. The day after my high school graduation, my mom became sick with a very high fever. Initially it was thought to be just a simple fever and no big deal, but it went on for days to weeks to months.

The first semester of college went by, just like that, and I was not a part of it. I was home caring for my mom, not knowing what the future held. It was quite possibly the most difficult time of my life—the fear of possibly losing my mom, the sadness of not being able to experience the beginning of college while watching all my friends leave home to do just that, coping with the sudden responsibility of running the entire household, and all the while I was only a teenager.

I began college during the spring semester, but I didn't really lose any time because I was able to place out of first year of college credit while still in high school. I had worked very hard in high school; receiving anything less than a 100 was unacceptable. I was the president of the Kiwanis Club and a National Honor society student; I won the best student award for every subject every year, received the president's recognition, and was in All State Choir and the top soprano of varsity choir, winning the best choir student award every year.

All these thoughts flashed before my eyes on my first day of college as I stood frozen in front of my classroom of 500 unfamiliar people who all seemed to know their way around. I had missed that initial part of college when everyone met for the first time. Even though I had more college credit than probably most students in that lecture hall, I felt behind and out of place. Growing up, I was a very shy girl. I didn't speak unless I was spoken to, not because I didn't want to but because I wasn't able to from my shyness. On this day, I felt outside my comfort zone and inside my nightmare, surrounded by strangers. I didn't eat lunch that day because having lunch meant going to a restaurant, ordering food by myself, and talking to a bunch of unknown people.

I went from being that unsure of myself and lacking that much self-confidence to becoming an invasive cardiologist; founder, CEO, and medical director of a cardiovascular institute; adjunct professor of medicine; and a founding director of the Global Health Alliance Foundation, where I work with world leaders. One of my biggest hurdles that I had to overcome was my own insecurities and lack of confidence. It took my entire medical training years to overcome this. College was not an easy time for me. My mom's health continued to be an issue all throughout college, which took an enormous toll on me. Hearing so many 'NO's along the way also did not help boost my confidence.

I attribute my success to a few core values that have carried me throughout all the hardships in my life. I recognized that I lacked confidence but not competence. I have always been an extremely hard-working person, and I focused on my skill and knowledge-building because knowledge equals power and confidence was only a matter of time. I wanted to be the best at what I did, as a way to compensate for my inability to speak up. I was tried and tested in every possible way in college, and despite all the hurdles that came my way, I managed to complete college and make it to medical school. I am grateful to my mentors for guiding me through my difficult times. A very powerful message came from my research mentor in college, Dr. Sata Sathasivan, who told me to take baby steps towards my goals and everything will be fine. I follow his advice to this day.

Medical school was a very challenging yet amazing journey for me, and I experienced tremendous personal growth during my four years. I will never forget my first day of medical school. We started gross anatomy on the very first day. I was really excited to start medical school, but there was one thing I was very anxious about and that was gross anatomy because I had a tremendous fear associated with dead bodies prior to medical school. I remember, as the secured double door to the anatomy lab opened to my class for the first time, there was dead silence; we were all in shock with the vision of a room full of cadavers awaiting us. I nervously approached my assigned tank. Everyone just stood there for the first five minutes; no one moved a muscle. I looked around at all my teammates and realized that I was not the only one afraid. Suddenly, I found the courage to take the first step; I picked up the scalpel and made the first incision, and my teammates followed.

Before I knew it, I was instructing and teaching anatomy to my teammates, not because I was better but because diving into it helped me overcome my fears. I was terrified the whole time but no one could tell. During anatomy rotation, I had taken many trips to the anatomy lab by myself sometimes even late at night working in a room full of cadavers alone to learn it better in preparation of exams. By the end of my anatomy rotation, something fascinating happened. My fear of dead bodies was completely gone, and I formed a unique bond with the cadaver I had the privilege of working with. I felt a sense of deep respect and appreciation for their contribution to medicine and my education. Just like my cadaver took my fear of dead bodies away, they also helped me to overcome my fear of going beyond my comfort zone. I found a new me, a more confident me.

I began to take on leadership roles, and during my second year of medical school I was elected as the president of the Student National Medical Association. I served as the president for two years, and during my tenure as the president, I established a number of things. I started a mentorship program for disadvantaged students at the local high school and at Texas Tech University for undergraduates who wanted to pursue medicine. I was placed in charge of improving diversity by the dean of the School of Medicine. I conducted a study at the medical school to assess any diversity issues. I then addressed it by creating a student committee to work directly with the admissions board and for the student body to have a voice in diversifying the medical school. I founded a scholarship endowment for underserved students, one of my biggest contributions to the medical school. I established a multicultural fundraising banquet to fund the scholarship that is now one of the biggest fundraising events in Lubbock, Texas; it has raised several hundred thousand dollars benefiting disadvantaged students and helping diversify the student body.

I can attest to this, through my personal experience, that if there is something you want to achieve in life, you have to set a goal and work hard while persevering towards that goal without giving up—no matter how many obstacles come your way—and nothing can stop you from achieving that.

Personal Success Story 4

Sriram Palepu, BSA, Biology and BBA Business Honors

Currently in Medical School at the University of Pennsylvania

Entering college can feel overwhelming at first. The struggle to meet new people and do well in classes is overshadowed by the larger career decisions that lie ahead. As a freshman, I remember thinking I had so much time to figure out what I wanted to do and how I wanted to get there. Before I even knew it, I was a junior applying to medical school and graduating a year later. I managed to figure out how to make the most of my college experience through a lot of mistakes and learning experiences. I hope to share a few of the things that worked for me so that you can better take advantage of your time in college-and set yourself up for later success.

1. Discover and solidify your interests through student organizations and classes.

Use your first few months as a freshman to explore activities and subjects you find interesting. Attend info sessions for student organizations. Sign up for a volunteer shift at an organization you are interested in learning more about. As a business student interested in environmental science, I explored a range of activities from a business fraternity to a community garden to cultural organizations and more. It is also important to be flexible. Some opportunities are competitive and may be hard to get into, so make sure to have several options.

2. Find your ideal working/relaxing ratio.

Everyone has a different working style. Some people like studying continuously for six hours and treating themselves to an hour-long break, while others like taking intermittent breaks. Some people like studying two weeks in advance, while others only need a few days. Understanding and developing your own study habits is crucial to being productive. Initially, I would try to copy my friends' study habits, which resulted in a lot of wasted time in the library. It was only in my sophomore year that I realized I like taking a fifteen-minute break every hour! Also, make sure to make time for social outings. Watching a movie, relaxing at the park, or planning a game night can really help prevent burnout!

3. Plan your degree early. It does not have to be set in stone.

It is important to have a rough idea of what classes you are taking each semester to graduate on time with all of the majors and certificates you want to do. I have many friends who had to drop a certificate, minor, or even major to graduate on time; some had to stay an extra semester to complete their requirements. While there is nothing wrong with taking extra time, a degree plan can help you prioritize certain classes and stay on track with career goals. As a freshman, I originally planned for a double major and two certificates. Throughout college, I dropped a major and removed some classes to accommodate taking the MCAT, a spring semester internship.

4. Narrow down activities to those that are meaningful.

While the beginning of college is about exploring your interests, the latter half of college is about "diving deep" and focusing on the activities that you resonate with the most. While taking on new positions, it is important to evaluate your time to prevent spreading yourself too thin. Take on extra responsibilities and apply for leadership positions in the activities you enjoy the most. For example, I started as a member of an environmental organization, then became an officer my sophomore year, and finally ran for president. At the same time, I dropped a business organization my freshman year as I focused more on my interests in health and environmental science. Of course, you can still actively look for new opportunities you find interesting. Do not be afraid to apply for a new opportunity you find interesting just because you are an upperclassman.

5. Think about the "next steps" for your career and set up a timeline!

All careers have certain timelines and requirements that students need to be mindful of. Whether you are recruiting for a job with your bachelor's degree or taking the GRE exam for graduate school, it is important to have a grasp over basic requirements. When I decided on applying to medical school,

I learned that I needed to take the MCAT and complete a year-long application process. I planned to give myself the summer of my junior year to study for the MCAT (take the test in August), and apply for medical school the following summer. Having a timeline of when you want to do the "big things" is helpful to getting them done on time. Unknowingly recruiting or taking a test (MCAT, NCLEX, LSAT, etc.) too late may cause you to fall behind or not be in the running for opportunities that go to early applicants. It is important to create realistic and practical checkpoints to reach your goals. Make sure to talk to mentors and upperclassmen in your field as well; their experiences and advice can help you better understand how to create your own plans. I hope these tips can help you make the most of your college experience!

Unit 3. Motivation

All our dreams can come true if we have the courage to pursue them.

Walt Disney

Chapter 7. Beyond Grades

Motivation to do well in any course is critical to succeed in not only that particular course but also to graduate from college. Just being smart but not going to class or studying the subject will not make you any smarter or help you succeed in college. While many students are motivated by grades as the main aim of education, the impact of education is far greater than getting good grades alone. When I did the survey of what motivates students in my biology class, the following picture emerges. This is from the Spring 2020 Introductory Biology I course for majors. The same patterns emerge almost every time I do this survey at the end of the semester, and the results may vary in another subject or course by another professor. Overall, the grade does matter, and it motivates the students as it may decide their future life or career goals, but not always.

There are many types of motivation essential for you to understand and use to your advantage. According to Ambrose et al., the two important concepts in understanding motivation are 1) the subjective value of a goal and 2) expectancies or the expectations of accomplishing that goal. A combination of these two will enable a goal-directed behavior, and the learning will be enhanced. If there is any mismatch in the subjective value of the goal between the student and the professor or if the expectations of the students do not meet the expectations of the professor, then there are obvious problems with the student not being motivated to work hard or study for success. Let us explore the details of these two aspects more.

What or who motivates you to do your best in this class? Select all that apply.

Answered: 332   Skipped: 8

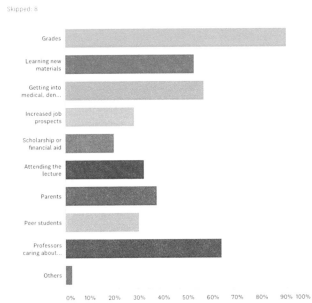

Figure 7.1 Factors that motivate a student to do their best in a biology course

The learning goals/objectives (before you learn) or learning outcomes (after you learn) are usually defined by the professors and are either given as a handout or part of the syllabus at the beginning of the semester or posted online in the learning management system (LMS). In addition, the professor may give additional review lists or actionable goals for each exam or orally mention them in class. Take these seriously, and try to understand in what level of detail the goals must be accomplished. Some professors get annoyed when the students ask them "Will this be on the exam?" Even though it seems to be a legitimate question, it shows that you are focused more on the exam and not on learning. Instead clarify the content with a slightly different question, such as "Should we remember the names of the scientists and years of these scientific experiments or just know the experiments themselves in detail?" This type of question implies you are fine with learning all of them but want to be more specific in understanding the learning goal. There is another aspect to this; as many students are used to digital media, they remain surface learners rather than deep learners, which the professors expect. So be clear as to what level of details you are supposed to know unless the professors explicitly state them.

Values are considered as "subjective value" because each of us differs in our value system, and what could be very interesting and valuable to one person may not have the same value for others. As summarized by Ambrose et al (2010), there are three types of values: attainment value, intrinsic value, and instrumental value. Attainment value is when the student has achieved the learning goal or the entire course; intrinsic value is the enjoyment during the learning process itself; and instrumental value is the accomplishment the course provides in addition to external benefits such as preparation for a competitive exam, praise, an opportunity to get a campus job or outside job, etc. Naturally, the more subjective values one has for a particular learning goal or the entire course the more motivated they will be to learn.

Expectancy or expectations are outcomes that learners need to believe they can actually do. If it is too difficult to attain the goal, the student may not feel motivated. If the professor provides sufficient instructions and resources to attain the learning goal, the student would feel much better about the expectancy of success and will be motivated to work on the assigned tasks. In addition, the environment needs to be conducive for the student to believe this is possible with the class being more nurturing than intimidating, such as with getting timely feedback from the professor.

As you can see from Figure 7.1, the second source of motivation for students who answered this survey are the professors who care about teaching, implying that such professors would work with or guide the students to accomplish the learning goals. Hence the course environment is also very critical to motivation. The source of encouragement or intimidation could also stem from fellow students who are willing to work with each other, communicate with each other respectfully, and support each other. In this aspect, having a study group or a support group, such as Freshmen Interest Groups (FIG) formed at the University of Texas at Austin or Freshmen Research Initiative (FRI), provides additional motivation to succeed. There are also student organizations dedicated to a professional career, such as premedical, predental, or prelaw, that can also be a source of motivation. In addition, the learning materials need to be relevant to the student's personal goals and real life.

Chapter 8. Health Matters

Without proper health in one's life, nothing else matters. There is a popular saying that health is wealth, and we have a golden opportunity to choose the right diet, exercise, habits, and rest to live a healthy life. Jimmy Carter once said "The awareness that health is dependent upon habits that we control makes us the first generation in history that to a large extent determines its own destiny." (https://proverbicals.com/health-proverbs) This is profoundly true; we are aware of most of the habits that would keep us either healthy or not so healthy.

College days can be the first time most students are away from home, taking care of themselves, eating in a cafeteria or cooking on their own, deciding when and what to eat, and forming exercise and sleep habits. The four years of college are very important and could be one of the best times of your life. Students have plenty of opportunities in college to take care of themselves with proper diet, exercise, and sleep. Gyms, sports facilities, and exercise classes are available in colleges for easy access and routine use.

Developing an exercise routine every day, with thirty to sixty minutes allocated for exercise from simple walking to intense workouts depending on what you are interested in, will add more energy and focus to your studies. It will also help reduce stress levels during exam times and increase the circulation of oxygen to boost energy levels. The Institute of Medicine (2013) published a detailed report through the National

Academies Press that showed physical activity improves academic performance in students.

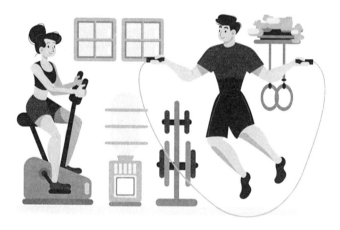

Figure 8.1 Exercise is important to keep body and mind healthy

In addition to physical health and exercise, mental health is also very important. The American College Health Association (2018) studied 40 post-secondary educational institutions and collected surveys from 26,181 students in the United States. They reported that 64 percent of students had experienced overwhelming anxiety during a twelve-month period and approximately 30 percent of students surveyed mentioned it negatively affected their academic performance. In the same report, 23 percent of college students who responded had been diagnosed with depression, and 18 percent of the respondents said depression negatively affected their academic performance. Paying attention to both physical and mental health during the college days is very important.

Test anxiety is another major issue, according to Linda O'Brien in her book, *How to Get Good Grades in College* (2009). She says starting early, practicing with sample exams, and doing proper body postures and breathing exercises can help reduce exam anxiety. Do not wait until things spiral out of control, and get necessary medical help as soon as possible. There are medical and academic counselors available to help, and informing professors about the medical situation also will help in flexible accommodation with assignments. Academic and health counselors can help with reaching out to professors if needed. In extenuating circumstances, there are provisions for non-academic withdrawal without affecting your grade point average. There may also be student organizations and support groups that may help if it is minor and you can handle it with peer support. There are some student organizations, such as MannMukti (https://www.mannmukti.org/) started at The University of Texas at Austin, that help bring awareness to mental health issues.

Time management and stress management are also essential to maintaining good health. The college class schedule is not structured similarly to high school, and you need to be prepared to make the best use of time to attend all the classes and not skip them, try and make it to the professor's office hours to ask questions on things you did not fully understand, attend any review sessions held in each class, and study before going to class and after coming back from the class. Make every hour and minute count. Take time to exercise, relax, and sleep well. Some of the success stories of students in this book also give you more ideas to consider in terms of time management. Avoid procrastinating with the assignment until the due date as you may not know whether the time allocated is sufficient. Start early and end slowly, or take all the time until the deadline. Watch for time drainers such as social media, watching random videos, and too much socialization. Realize your main goal of attending college is to learn, get the best education possible, and graduate. Anything that distracts from your mission needs to be carefully considered and avoided.

Try to maintain a check list for each day and week so you can maximize the outputs in each day to be productive. Include time to relax but not waste. Utilize all the resources provided by the professor and the institution. Utilize the time between classes effectively; try to avoid napping in the afternoon as it might interrupt the flow of your activities and interfere with your regular night sleep pattern. If you become too tired while studying, vary the activity to something physical such as walking, cleaning your room, or doing your laundry. There are many more simple tips for time management and study management in Cal Newport's *How to Win at College* (2005).

Stress management is another skill that you might want to master whether by doing meditation, walking around the campus, talking to your friends or doing breathing exercise or yoga. In addition, develop a perspective on life; prioritize what is the most important for you and don't sweat the small stuff. Develop a circle of friends with whom you can share and help each other, whether through the Freshmen Interest Group, a laboratory research group, a professional student organization, or a sports activity. If all things don't work, don't hesitate to seek a counselor's advice or talk to a professor you trust and who cares about you.

Chapter 9. True Grit

Mastering the content, learning study skills, and being motivated may still not be enough unless we have the patience and perseverance to succeed. You may have heard of the rabbit and the tortoise story where the tortoise was slow and steady but persisted all the way to win the race. Academic life is not very different than that story. Angela Duckworth (2016) wrote the classic book *Grit—The Power of Passion and Perseverance* from her landmark research exploring what makes people successful in difficult tasks. Starting from West Point Academy, she studied successful businesspeople, athletes winning in Olympics, and successful students. Her book is one of the suggested readings listed at the end of this book.

Duckworth points out it is not just the SAT or ACT scores or your GPA that helps you succeed in life; the passion you have for your work and your perseverance until you succeed are just as important. Is it something innate in us or something that can be cultivated? As she elaborates, grit can be cultivated from the inside out with an interest that transforms into passion, followed by hard work and practice with a clear purpose of accomplishment or becoming something with the optimistic hope you will get there. Such grit can also be nurtured by parents and teachers when they identify a talent in a student to guide them, support them, and provide all the feedback and encouragement possible.

When you are in college you have several opportunities to choose a major, choose the courses within the major, and work hard to accomplish your goals to eventually make an A or graduate from college. Many students don't have a clear idea of what they are sincerely passionate about; unless you try various things that are interesting to you how can you settle on the one thing that you would love to do for the rest of your life? Even when you know what you are passionate about, there may not be any career opportunities in that field or the competition is so high it will take an enormous effort to accomplish your goal. Sometimes, you need to reconsider your goals, but once you know the purpose clearly you can develop the passion and perseverance to succeed. I have seen students who made an A in the first exam and the started slacking by not coming to class or skipping assignments finally ending up with a C while someone who made a B or C in the first exam, visited my office hours, asked me how they can improve, worked hard at it, and finally ended up making an A or A- with all the drops and curves at the end of the semester. Having overconfidence is not going to help you. You need to have an open mind and curiosity to learn new things in life and experience various options before settling on one to pursue as your passion. Having a growth mindset and perseverance will help you take feedback constructively and accomplish your learning goals.

Having true grit is great, but there are occasions when you need to be persistent but smart if you have options about classes and the ways you can accomplish the same goal. When you are starting with various courses, there are some professors whose expectations and instructional methods are unfair or unreasonable; you don't have to stick to the same class because you are not a quitter or you have the grit. If you have a choice of moving to a better professor who will offer a more conducive environment to help you learn the same subject matter without compromising on the quality, you ought to consider them, and it is just fine to make the switch on time.

Figure 9.1 Reaching your goal takes persistent efforts

Patience is a virtue when you feel frustrated about not being able to master certain content and you feel stuck. There are so many resources you can access by not only asking your professor or teaching assistant but also at the learning centers where tutors are available. Having hope and a growth mindset will help you sustain the interest and find ways to overcome difficult situations in any course. Even though many parents may be concerned about their student's wellbeing and course grades, and are willing to go to any length to help them succeed, some parents may not have had the college experience or time to offer much help. In either case, you want to take your own responsibility to learn and find ways to be an independent learner. This will help you in the long run.

Accepting failures and mistakes is also a virtue so long as you can learn from it and pick yourself up to succeed after each failure. This also leads to developing that grit. Over time you will become resourceful to find solutions to almost every problem that you face in your classes. Having the passion and a purpose will also help maintain your grit. Sometimes I have one or two students come to me during the last week of the semester asking for help. I still talk to them but advise that they should have started asking for help early in the semester so they could better understand why they are not performing well and how to improve. Timely and specific feedback is very important so do not wait until it is too late to improve your chances of success in each course.

During your four years of college, visit your academic advisors as often as possible to understand the degree program requirements, set the sequence of courses you need to take, and form a schedule to accomplish those degree requirements. Then you can break that into freshmen, sophomore, junior, and senior years and into semesters in each year. Once you have that degree program and schedule ready, start the planning early to take the best possible classes and professors and identify resources to help when you need them to do well in every course that you take. Having that vision of what it takes to complete your degree will give you the patience and perseverance to sustain the long haul and strategize to win in college.

Personal Success Story 5

Omar Vayani, BSA. Biochemistry, Honors

Currently in University of Chicago Pritzker School of Medicine

Growing up, my parents and family were extremely supportive of my interests. They came to this country as immigrants and endured a struggle that allowed me to explore my passions both in and outside of school. Part of me always knew that medicine was the route for me because of the many personal experiences I had while growing up. I eventually realized that having the ability to leverage scientific knowledge and discovery to enhance someone else's life would be very rewarding for me. Additionally, I knew that this career would forge a way for me to learn from the experiences of many individuals. With these thoughts in mind, I was able to manifest an internal drive that has thankfully allowed me to become a medical student and future physician. Getting here was never easy. I had to make mistakes and learn from them over and over again before I made it to where I am today. And although I still have a long way to go, I want to share some personal tips and strategies that have helped me over the years:

Establish a strong support system. I believe that a strong support system is one of the most important things you can do to be successful. The beauty of college is that many people have similar interests and goals as you. In this type of environment, you are bound to find individuals that can serve as your closest supporters and help you grow. For me, it was important to find people who would help me become the best version of myself, people that would not only enhance me academically but also personally. Because I was living away from home, I wanted to find a family of friends that I could go to in both moments of difficulty and happiness. Doing this and finding these people, improved my college experience in ways that I could not have ever imagined. I've always heard that you are the combination of the people closest to you. In other words, you are a representation of the values, experiences, and personalities of the people you choose to surround yourself with. Find people who have qualities that you want to emulate. Whether it is their demeanor or academic excellence, having people in your life that teach you through the way they live is extremely important to your success.

Don't compare yourself to others. This is a big one. It may sound cliché, but everyone is on their own timeline. We live in a society that, unfortunately, equates personal value to social media likes and followers. This mentality very easily bleeds into everyday work. It's important to realize that you're not alone. Guess what? That person who seems to be amazing at everything and has perfect grades is also probably struggling. This doesn't mean you shouldn't be competitive. A little healthy competition between friends is a great way to advance yourself. But don't ever invest your own emotional well-being into how you are doing in comparison to someone else. This is something I struggled with a lot during the early parts of my undergrad. I quickly learned, however, that this toxic mentality would only make me feel worse about myself. Instead, I've been learning to look at the bigger picture of where I am on my own journey. I try to remind myself every day of my talents and the potential I have to succeed. You should do the same. Celebrate yourself and your strengths. Work hard to become the best version of yourself. You are worth it!

3. **Explore your interests and find your passion.** I cannot stress this enough. Sometimes we get caught up in doing what we "think" we should be doing versus what we should actually be doing. College is a time to explore yourself and things that make you happy. Find that one thing that brightens your mood and gives you warmth. During my time at UT, I involved myself in activities that fulfilled me. From undergraduate teaching to volunteering with refugee families, I sought out experiences that gave me different perspectives on this world. In doing so, I was able to make connections with people that enriched my life with new lessons every day. This also applies to interests outside of school. It is so important to try new things to grow as an individual. So go out and try that new hobby, read that book, and experience a new culture. This will only help you in the long run.

4. **Talk to your professors!** Contrary to what your high school teachers may tell you, your college professors care about you

and your success. While there may be some who are not this way, there are also many who are willing to be there for you through everything. From my own experience, some of my professors have been the most invested and caring individuals I have ever met. Their guidance both in and outside the classroom is something that has helped me get to where I am today. If you need a reminder or just someone to help you see the bigger picture, go to these individuals. They've led lives filled with many of the things you are going through. Their experience can only make yours better!

Care about yourself. Many people fail to acknowledge this point. And that is to look out for your mental health and well-being. In this stage of life, you are likely to be very independent. This can be a good and a bad thing. There are probably fewer people looking after you and that means that you are your own caretaker. College was the time for me to establish healthy habits and hobbies that helped me maintain myself emotionally and mentally. Along with my support system, I also enjoyed things like working out, watching Netflix, and cooking. You owe it to yourself to have days where you unwind from the stresses of your academic and professional life. The time that you spend rejuvenating and refreshing yourself is never a waste. Self-care can only help improve your work ethic and prevent burnout. Love yourself!

Don't be afraid to get back up. There will be times on this journey when you will feel like you have failed. Whether it is in the first month or in two years, I promise that a time will come when you will be forced to re-evaluate your strategy and start again. That is okay and that is normal. It's important to look at the big picture while also condensing your goals into manageable steps. Realize why you are doing what you are doing. Revisit your intentions. This will help you find that drive to start again. And continue to use the above strategies. I know they have helped me immensely, and I hope they will do the same for you!

Personal Success Story 6

Sailesh Kumar, BS. Computer Science Honors

Senior Software Engineer at Facebook

 It's truly remarkable to think about how fluid time is; how things seem like they last forever in the moment, and then life just moves on. I remember going through extremely stressful times in high school and college, studying for tests, working on job applications and college applications, etc. Each time I told myself that once I achieved that milestone (a job at Facebook, getting into a top 10 computer science university, etc.), I'd be set for life. Each time I was wrong.

The reason I am talking about this is to fully highlight what I believe to be the key to succeeding in school, and beyond. I think too many of us have conditional and externally driven motivation that either burns us out or leaves us seeking greater meaning. Life is extremely long, and we can't fool ourselves into thinking we'll have it all figured out in the beginning.

But, with that mentality, if we focus on the long game, how can we be productive and succeed? The sustainable solution for me has been to speed up the micro but slow down the macro. Focus on your mental health, and find ways to engage your passions and your creative side. In college I helped start a mental health organization called MannMukti. Doing so has made me so much more cognizant of the choices I make that impact my mental health and my success in various ventures. It opened my eyes to how much we set ourselves up for success, or for failure, based on the people we surround ourselves with, the content we consume, and the thoughts we feed our minds. I encourage everyone to reflect on what they do that brings out the best in themselves and what they do that brings out the worst. Constantly reflect and check in on yourself, and you'll slowly be able to make changes to elevate your best, and minimize your worst.

The other piece of advice I have for you is on efficiency. When I think back to my undergraduate career, there are a lot of things I would do differently. The biggest mistake I made was misplacing my work and time. Would you rather show up to class and not pay attention and then have to stress and cram at the end for the final? Or would you show up to class and just learn it there, while accompanied and guided by a literal expert in the field? The answer is obvious, but yet I consciously chose the worse option.

I spent Fall 2019 as an adjunct professor at Georgia State, and experiencing the undergraduate experience from that side blew my mind. Students who paid attention in class did better. Students who showed up to office hours did better. You and I might say "duh!" but I often had to pay the price to catch up in class. While I did well, it was not as efficient as it could be.

These two pieces of advice go hand in hand. As we slowly introduce and solidify new habits in our lives, we will be able to spend more time being productive, and be more productive with the time we spend. This is a sure-fire way to become a high functioning individual and to succeed at the highest level. If you're reading this book that means you already care about your success and are looking to reflect and improve, which is already a step in the right direction. Keep on reflecting and improving, and you'll find yourself at great heights before you know it. Good luck!

Conclusion

There are three academic aspects that directly impact the success of students in a particular course or in graduating from college. The first and foremost is knowledge. The preparations that students start college with and how they can help build new knowledge are important. Learning the big picture and the bottom line of learning objectives or goals will help guide you to succeed in a course. Teaching styles and expectations are different from professor to professor, and the student should learn to adapt to all different styles.

The second aspect covered is study skills; these will help you to understand how the learning process works in terms of both cognitive psychology and the evidence-based principles of learning. The discussion on Bloom's taxonomy in its modern version will help you understand and analyze how the learning framework is structured and how you can use it to your advantage and succeed.

Lastly, the motivation aspect is an essential component affected by the subjective values and expectancies of both professors and students. Motivation is essential for anyone to succeed. Both physical and mental health are important to succeed in anything and are very important in college as one becomes a more and more independent and self-directed learner.

In addition to developing strong academic knowledge and practical skills, gain some real-life experience with volunteer work, a part-time job (if you can manage the time), a summer internship, study abroad, or participating in student organizations to develop leadership skills. Also, develop soft skills such as team work skills, communication skills, and interviewing skills.

Additional resources are provided at the end and are updated regularly online at Squarecap Academy's section on Ensuring Academic Success & Your Graduation. Visit SquarecapAcademy.us for more information. In summary, remember why you started college and what your life ambitions are; find ways to make them happen. Passion and persistence go a long way once you are committed to your life's mission.

References and Recommended Readings

Ambrose, Susan A., Bridges, Michael W., Dipietro, Michele, Lovett, Marsha C., and Norman, Marie K. (2010). *How Learning Works – 7 Research based Principles for Smart Teaching.* John Whiley & Sons. San Francisco, California.

American College Health Association Report (2018) downloaded from https://www.acha.org/documents/ncha/NCHA-II_Fall_2018_Reference_Group_Executive_Summary.pdf

Bloom's Taxonomy. Adapted from Center for Teaching at The Vanderbilt University. https://cft.vanderbilt.edu/guides-sub-pages/blooms-taxonomy/

Brown, Jeff and Fenske, Mark, with Neporent, Liz. (2010). *The Winners Brain – 8 Strategies Great Minds Use to Achieve Success.* Harvard University Press. Cambridge, Massachusetts.

Brown, Peter C., Roediger III, Henry L., and McDaniel, Mark A. (2014). *Make It Stick – The Science of Successful Learning.* The Belknap Press of Harvard University Press. Cambridge, Massachusetts.

Browning, Geil. (2006). *Emergenetics – Tap into the New Science of Success.* Harper Collins Books. New York, New York.

Burger, Edward B. and Starbird, Michael. (2012). *The Five Elements of Effective Thinking.* Princeton University Press. Princeton, New Jersey.

Colvin, Geoff. (2010). *Talent is Overrated – What Separates World Class Performers from Everybody Else.* Penguin Group. Simon & Schuster Inc., New York, New York.

Dehaene, Stanislas. (2020). *How We Learn – Why Our Brains Learn Better Than Any Machine…for Now.* Viking, An Imprint or Penguin Random House LLC., New York, New York.

Duckworth, Angela. (2016). *Grit -The Power of Passion and Perseverance.* Simon & Schuster Inc., New York, New York.

Farber, Alan. (2013). *College Success 1- and 2-Year Programs.* Woodburn Press, Dayton, Ohio.

Forehand, M. (2005). Bloom's Taxonomy: Original and Revised. In M. Orey (Ed.), Emerging Perspectives on Learning, Teaching, and Technology (E-Book). https://textbookequity.org/Textbooks/Orey_Emergin_Perspectives_Learning.pdf.

Freire, Paulo.(1999). *Pedagogy of the Oppressed*. Continuum
Publishing Company, New York, New York.

Gall, Meredith D. and Gall, Joyce P. (1985). *Study for Success*. M
Damien Publishers, Eugene, Oregon.

Gladwell, Malcolm. (2008). *Outliers - The Story of Success*. Little
Brown and Company. New York, New York.

Newport, Cal. (2005) *How to Win in College*. Broadway Books. New
York, New York.

O'Brien, Linda. (2009). *How to Get Good Grades in College*.
Woodburn Press, Dayton, Ohio.

Ripley, Amanda. (2013). *The Smartest Kids in the World and How
They Got That Way*. Simon & Schuster Inc., New York, New
York.

Tough, Paul. (2019). *The Years That Matter the Most – How College
Makes or Breaks Us*. Houghton Mifflin Harcourt. New York,
New York.

Walker, Matthew. (2017). *Why We Sleep – Unlocking the Power of
Sleep and Dreams*. Scribner. An Imprint of Simon & Schuster
Inc., New York, New York.

Wagner, Tony. (2012). *Creating Innovators – The Making of Young People Who Will Change the World*. Scribner. An Imprint of Simon & Schuster Inc., New York, New York.

Weinstein, Yana and Sumeracki, Megan, with Caviglioli, Oliver. (2019). *Understanding How We Learn*. A David Fulton Book by Rutledge, A Taylor Francis Group. New York, New York.

APPENDIX

Sample of Exam Wrapper

Learning skills can be improved through self-reflection. This "exam wrapper" is a self-reflection tool for you to use and keep. This is an iterative process, and try to be as objective as possible. Developed by K. Sata Sathasivan with inputs from other biology faculty at The University of Texas at Austin.

Part A. Multiple Choice grade _____%

Multiple choice A	A. Didn't remember the necessary facts	B. Didn't understand the necessary concepts	C. Was unable to apply the concepts	D. Made a simple mistake or misread question	E. Correct, no problem!
1					
2					
3					
4					
5					
6					
7					
8					
9					
10					
11					
12					
13					
14					
15					
16					
17					

18				
19				
20				
21				
22				
23				
24				
25				
TOTAL				

Part B. Free response questions _____%

Written answers	A. Didn't **remember** the necessary facts	B. Didn't **understand** the necessary concepts	C. Was unable to **apply** the concepts	D. Made a simple **mistake** or **misread** question	E. Correct, **no problem**!
1.					
2					
3					
4					
5					
6					
7					
8					
9					
10					
TOTAL					

B. Consider the following self-reflection statements about course-work

Learning Activity	Totally True	Mostly True	Kind of True	Not True
I read something about the topic in the textbook before coming to class.				
I read the textbook a little bit at a time, then put it away and try to summarize in writing what I learned.				
I prepare to learn before each class by looking over my notes from the previous class.				
I make note of the concepts that I do not fully understand during lecture and try to clear them up for myself using the textbook or in discussion section.				
I use the Learning Outcome handouts to test my knowledge and practice writing answers without notes.				
I use concept maps, diagrams, flow charts, and tables to learn and organize the information.				
I complete the weekly self-quizzes by myself, after I think I'm prepared, and treat them as practice exams.				
I begin studying in advance for the exam and give myself enough time to learn the material.				
I visit the office hours of the professor or TA and attended the review sessions.				
Other study methods: (Briefly describe)				

C. Answer the following statements:

The study methods that were helpful to me in taking this exam are as follows:

For the next exam, I'm going to try the following new study methods:

Concept Maps: What, Why, and How

Samraat Pawar and K. Sata Sathasivan

What is a concept map?

It is a diagram that shows how ideas are organized and related. It shows the content in a structured, hierarchical manner, typically with the simplest concepts/idea at one end and the most complex/inclusive/general ones at the other. Such maps can be used as a study tool as well as a teaching tool (to explain stuff to your classmates).

Why should I make concept maps?

In this course, you will make better progress if you develop concept maps covering different parts of the syllabus, either as an individual or *as a group* (recommended). Studying biology means studying levels of organization ranging from atoms to ecosystems. In BIO 311c, we will be going from atoms to cellular organization and function. There is a lot of material to remember, a lot of pieces of information to put together, and therefore you need to organize your knowledge in a logical, structured order (or hierarchy). From the perspective of this course in particular, this help you in three main ways:

   i. Remembering and understanding key terms better.
  ii. Developing your understanding so that you can solve problems (instead of merely recalling stuff).
 iii. As you see the big picture, and how it is made of small parts, you will feel more confident about and interested in the subject.

Remember, most details of each concept can be reconstructed from the map, reducing the load on memory and reducing memorization errors.

How do I/we make a concept map?
Here are some key steps:
(1) Survey the problem carefully to understand what levels of complexity it covers. Read relevant passages of your lecture notes, course readings, and the textbook, trying to comprehend as much as possible.
(2) Select the most important or inclusive concept/idea/term in the content, to which all other concepts/ideas/terms can be related or subsumed under it. Write this inclusive concept/idea/term at the top and center of your page.
(3) Make list of terms/concepts by rereading your study material. Identify words that stand for key concepts (by circling or underlining them), and/or list them on a separate sheet.
(4) Rank the concepts/ideas/terms hierarchically, from the most inclusive to the least inclusive.
(5) Using boxes (or circles) and arrows (to indicate relationships), arrange the concepts/terms in a logical order to form a tree-like structure, starting with the most general/inclusive/complex ones at the top (or at the center), and the most. simple/fundamental/specific ones at the bottom (or around the central concept/idea/term)
(6) Write one or more words reflecting the relationships between concepts/terms next to the connecting arrows or lines.

(7) <u>Write down relevant examples</u> at each level of the map. *At the very least, these examples should include the ones covered in the lectures and discussion sections.*

(8) <u>Review your concept map</u>. Can you add other information? Can you think of another way that your map can be better developed?

(9) <u>Write one or more paragraphs summarizing the concept map</u>. The summary should include sources of information if you need to look up details of any concept/idea/term. Such sources may include course materials (lecture notes, readings, etc.), internet web pages, etc.

If there is any single most useful warning that can be given about concept maps, it is this: *do not put in too much information.* Concept maps are meant to show the relationships between key terms or concepts. So there is no point in including too many details. If your map looks more frightening than the textbook, there is something wrong!

Is there a "perfect" map?

No! There is no single correct map. Concept mapping is a creative process, during which you learn not just the information content but also how to map itself! You will get better as you do concept maps more often. You should compare and contrast your maps with those of your peers; this will really help you make rapid improvements.

EXAMPLE

Make a **concept map** of biological molecules. Start with Carbohydrates, Lipids, Proteins, and Nucleic acids on the top and the specific examples at the bottom. There will be three or four levels of this concept map. Include the monomers in each group and the types of bonds in each macromolecule (underline or highlight the macromolecules only).

Biological Molecules

Groups: Carbohydrates   Lipids   Proteins   Nucleic Acids

Subgroups

Examples

Monomers

Bond-connecting
Monomers

Draw one monomer for each group.

BLOOM'S TAXONOMY UPDATED VERSION
Action Verbs

Adapted from Anderson, L.W, and Krathwohl, 2001. "A Taxonomy for Learning, Teaching and Assessing".
An abridged edition. Allyn & Bacon, Boston, MA. By K. Sathasivan, 2020

Factual Knowledge		Conceptual Knowledge	Procedural Knowledge		Metacognitive Knowledge
Remembering	Understanding	Applying	Analyzing	Evaluating	Creating
Arrange	Classify	Add	Analyze	Argue	Assemble
Define	Compare	Allocate	Appraise	Assess	Assimilate
Describe	Confirm	Alter	Associate	Attack	Categorize
Detail	Contrast	Apply	Break down	Compare & contrast	Collect
Draw	Convert	Calculate	Criticize	Conclude	Combine
Duplicate	Decipher	Change	Discern	Critique	Compile
Identify	Defend	Choose	Diagram	Debate	Compose
Indicate	Designate	Complete	Discriminate	Decide	Condense
Label	Differentiate	Compute	Dissect	Deduce	Construct
List	Equate	Conduct	Distinguish	Diagnose	Create
Locate	Estimate	Coordinate	Elect	Evaluate	Design
Match	Examine	Demonstrate	Establish	Forecast	Derive
Name	Express	Determine	Explain	Improve	Develop
Outline	Extrapolate	Direct	Expound	Judge	Devise
Pick	Generalize	Discover	Illustrate	Justify	Elaborate
Point	Give examples	Divide	Inspect	Measure	Expand
Pronounce	Group	Dramatize	Profile	Prioritize	Generate
Quote	Infer	Draw	Question	Prove	Guide
Recall	Interpret	Employ	Refute	Rank	Hypothesize
Recite	Order	Formulate	Separate	Rate	Improve
Recognize	Paraphrase	Gather	Simplify	Recommend	Innovate
Record	Predict	Graph	Subdivide	Resolve	Integrate
Relate	Rephrase	Make	Summarize	Revise	Invent
Repeat	Rewrite	Manipulate	Test	Select	Manage
Reproduce	Sort	Model		Solve	Modify
Restate	Specify	Multiply		Support	Organize
State	Substitute	Operate		Value	Plan
Underline	Tell	Perform		Verify	Prepare
	Translate	Present		Weigh	Prescribe
		Provide			Produce
		Recount			Propose
		Report			Rearrange
		Schedule			Reconstruct
		Show			Reorganize
		Sketch			Rework
		Subtract			Set up
		Use			Synthesize
		Utilize			Theorize
					Transform
					Write